JOHANN SEBASTIAN BACH

CONCERTO FOR PIANO (HARPSICHORD), FLUTE AND VIOLIN S. 1044

BRANDENBURG CONCERTO NO. 5 IN D MAJOR

3057

COMPACT DISC PAGE AND BAND INFORMATION

MMO CD 3057

Music Minus One

JOHANN SEBASTIAN BACH

CONCERTO FOR PIANO (HARPSICHORD), FLUTE AND VIOLIN
BRANDENBURG CONCERTO NO. 5 IN D MAJOR

Printed in Canada

JOHANN SEBASTIAN BACH
CONCERTO FOR PIANO (HARPSICHORD), FLUTE AND VIOLIN
IN A MINOR

S. 1044

MMOCD 3057

* The small notes are to be played

4

A Solo

MMOCD 3057

tap

poco meno mosso

Tutti

12

Adagio ma non tanto, e dolce ♪ - 60

tap tap tap

Solo

I **Tutti**

tap

tap

L Solo

tap

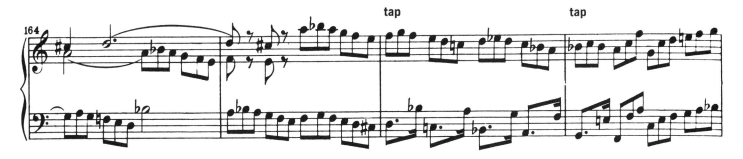

tap   tap

M

Cadenza - allow 25 seconds to taps

(Tempo 1) Tutti

MMOCD 3057

JOHANN SEBASTIAN BACH
BRANDENBURG CONCERTO NO. 5 IN D MAJOR

Cadenza - allow 3 minutes 5 seconds to taps

Solo

207

209

211

213

215

(cresc)

218

tap   tap

(f)

223

(rit.)

MMOCD 3057

MUSIC MINUS ONE 50 Executive Boulevard • Elmsford New York 10523-1325